TUR

Uses & Medicinal Prop of the Wonderful Herb

●

Dr. Rajeev Sharma

MANOJ PUBLICATIONS

© *All Rights Reserved*

Publishers :

Manoj Publications

761, Main Road, Burari, Delhi-110084
Ph.: 27611116, 27611349, Fax: 27611546
Mobile: 9868112194
E-mail: *info@manojpublications.com*
(For online shopping visit our website)
Website: *www.manojpublications.com*

Showroom :

Manoj Publications

1583-84, Dariba Kalan, Chandni Chowk,
Delhi-110006
Ph.: 23262174, 23268216, Mobile: 9818753569

ISBN : 978-81-310-0740-2
Fifth Edition : 2014

₹ 50

Printers :
Jai Maya Offset
Jhilmil Industrial Area, Delhi-110095

Turmeric : Dr. Rajeev Sharma

PREFACE

Besides flavouring food, to purify the blood and skin conditions remedy is probably the most common use of turmeric. Indians have known the magical medicinal properties of turmeric for ages. Ayurveda used it for the treatment of many inflammatory conditions and diseases like arthritis and muscular disorders. It was also used to tackle asthma, flatulence, colic and ringworm.

Medical research has recently shown that turmeric could halt the spread of breast cancer to the lungs apart from improving the effectiveness of ongoing medication. It has been seen that turmeric has high dose of curcumin that is an antidote to breast cancer.

Turmeric in India is always considered a magical herb. Indian folklore had always said that turmeric helped reduce inflammation. It is used as a blood purifier, anti-oxidant, anti-inflammatory, expectorant and skin tonic. It is used to treat measles, cough, sprains, and scabies.

Turmeric is also used in the production of sunscreens. In India, it is a common practice to smear turmeric paste on the outer skin of a bride, as it is believed to be a good cosmetic giving a glow to the skin and destroying bacteria.

In this book the subject is covered to its full. We try our best to cover every aspect of turmeric, its medicinal and industrial use along with home remedies.

—*Publishers*

CONTENTS

TURMERIC—INTRODUCTION

Turmeric is one of the most popular spice of India. It is also popular as medicine popularly used as part of home remedy. Almost in every dish prepared in India turmeric is added. Further, it is also regarded by the Hindus as something 'sacred' for use in ceremonial and religious functions. The spice turmeric or *Haldi* consists of the dried, boiled, cleaned and polished rhizomes (the underground swollen stem of the plant) of Turmeric plant.

Botanical name : Curcuma longa Linn.
Curcuma domestica Val.
Curcuma aromatica Linn.
Family name : Zingiberaceae.

Indian names are as follows:
Hindi : Haldi
Bengali : Halud, Pitarus
Gujarati : Haldhar, Haldi
Kannada : Arishina
Konkani : Halad
Malayalam : Manjal
Marathi : Halad, Halede
Oriya : Haladi
Punjabi : Haldar, Haldhar, Haldi
Sanskrit : Haladi, Haridra, Harita
Tamil : Manjal
Telugu : Pasupu
Urdu : Haladi

Under the genus Curcuma, to which turmeric belongs, the botanists have so far recognized 30 varieties. Of these,

Curcuma longa is economically the most important accounting for about 96.4% of the total area under turmeric and the remaining 3.6% of the total area are cultivated under Curcuma aromatica, which is mostly grown in small areas in Andhra Pradesh and Tamil Nadu.

Curing of raw turmeric rhizomes freshly dug out of earth is essential both for the development of the attractive yellow colour, mostly due to a pigment called curcumin, and characteristic aroma, as without it turmeric's lacks demand. The fingers and bulbs are boiled separately in water for half an hour until froth and white fumes appear. They are then drained and dried in the sun for 10 to 15 days until they become dry and hard. At this stage, the fingers produce a metallic sound, when broken in hand. They are then cleaned and polished mechanically in a drum rotated by hand or by power. Improved method of curing has been developed by CFTRI, Mysore which ensures better quality of end product.

Most of the turmeric produced in India is utilized as condiment. Only a small fraction is used in medicine, cosmetics and in dyeing of textile. The quality attributes of the commercial produce are its appearance in colour, maturity, bulk density, length and thickness, intensity of colour of the core and aroma etc. Turmeric produced in different areas is known by various local names. There are 16 such local varieties. Besides, the AGMARK Grades have been framed for (i) Turmeric fingers, (ii) Bulbs and (iii) Powder, separately both for export and for internal trade.

Turmeric has the following composition :

Moisture : 5.8%   Protein : 8.6%

Fat : 8.9%   Carbohydrates : 63.0%

Fiber : 6.9%   Total ash : 6.8%

Calcium : 0.2%   Phosphorus : 0.26%

Iron : 0.05%   Sodium : 0.01%

Potassium : 2.5%

Vitamin A (carotene) : 175 I.U./100 gram

Vitamin B_1 : 0.09 mg/100 gram

Vitamin B_2 : 0.19 mg/100 gram

Vitamin C (ascorbic acid) : 49.8 mg/100 gram

Niacin : 4.8 mg/100 gram.

Calorific value (food energy) : 390 calories/100 grams.

□□

THE MAGIC OF TURMERIC

The world today is discovering the magic of turmeric. Indians knew it all along. Worldwide research is now validating the medicinal properties of the root. In a quiet corner of Noida, the most modern town of Uttar Pradesh in India, scientists have discovered that turmeric has properties that can help fight cancer.

If your grandma put a pinch of turmeric powder into her cooking everyday, it was with good reason. It was not just to give the bright yellow glow to food. It was her best antidote for you. You will rarely see an Indian kitchen without a can of turmeric powder on the shelves. Most of us think it is used in our cooking as curcumin; the bright yellow pigment in the root gives colour to the food. But Ayurveda, the ancient form of Indian medicine, had recognized it to be a body cleanser having multiple medicinal properties. Scientific investigations are now showing that it can cure a host of diseases.

Indians have known the magical medicinal properties of turmeric for ages. Ayurveda used it for the treatment of many inflammatory conditions and diseases like arthritic and muscular disorders. It was also used to tackle asthma, flatulence, colic and ringworm.

But today, the versatility of turmeric in combating a number of complex diseases like cancer and multiple sclerosis is amazing scientists abroad. A study by The American Association for Cancer Research in San Francisco, California, shows that turmeric could help lower the risk of cancer. Researchers found in laboratory tests that curcumin can enhance the cancer fighting power in treatment if combined with TRAIL, a naturally occurring molecule that helps kill cancer cells.

A study at the University of Texas, Arlington showed that turmeric helped prevent cancer with its anti-oxidant properties. Kathryn Grant and Craig Schneider from the University of Arizona found in clinical trails that turmeric could improve morning stiffness, walking time and swelling in patients with rheumatoid arthritis.

Closer home, scientists at the Institute of Cytology and Preventive Oncology (ICPO) based in Noida, Uttar Pradesh, have recently found that curcumin protects the body from the deadly Human Papilloma Virus (HPV) that is the main cause for cervical cancer. This is how curcumin works—Certain HPV viruses need viral oncogine protein from cells in the body to express themselves rapidly. Curcumin actually stops the protein from epithelial cells to bind with the virus. Clinical trails of the compound have already started in the All India Institute of Medical Sciences, Chittaranjan National Cancer Institute, Tata Memorial Hospital and ICPO. The trails will cost over a crore of rupees and will be financed by the department of biotechnology and the Indian Council of Medical Research. Results are expected to take over three years.

Director General of Indian Council of Agricultural Research points out that as turmeric has got so many medicinal properties and will be a very paying proposition in the years to come and there would naturally be an international interest.

International interest in the neuro-protective potential of turmeric has risen after seeing its efficacy in traditional treatment in India. Over 90 scientific institutions in the United States are today studying the magical medical properties of the ancient Indian herb. Many of them are specifically studying how turmeric can inhibit growth of various types of cancer.

The University of Arizona is using a multi-million dollar

U.S. government grant to study turmeric's anti-inflammatory activities. Its team has shown that turmeric could prevent joint inflammation in rats. It has raised hopes of a cure for arthritis and osteoporosis patients that suffer a lot in their later years.

Medical research has recently shown that turmeric could halt the spread of breast cancer to the lungs apart from improving the effectiveness of ongoing medication. It has been seen that turmeric has high does of curcumin that is an antidote to breast cancer. Preliminary tests on mice have already been carried out in England.

How does turmeric work? Curcumin works by shutting down a protein active in the spread of breast cancer. More interestingly, it is also now believed to even reverse a side effect of commonly prescribed chemotherapy whose prolonged use may actually help to spread the disease. Curcumin breaks down the dose, making the therapy less toxic.

Japanese researchers at the Hamamatsu University School of Medicine say that turmeric may help cure colitis that leads to inflammation of the intestines. A preliminary study at the Vanderbilt University in Nashville, Tennessee has shown that turmeric may arrest the progression of multiple sclerosis that is an incurable disease affecting the brain.

A senior scientist formerly at the National Institute of Science Communication says that scientists in the United States are today proving in labs what Indian traditional knowledge knew for ages. Potent molecules derived from nature and medicinal plants that were traditionally used will show wonders in newer and newer diseases in the future. Such experiments validate doubts that the intellect questions about traditional medicine.

India produces nearly the whole world's crop of turmeric. It uses 80 per cent of the produce, as it is an important ingredient in Indian cooking occupying a pride of place on every kitchen shelf.

Turmeric in India was always considered a magical herb. Indian folklore had always said that turmeric helped reduce inflammation. It was used as a blood purifier, anti-oxidant, anti-inflammatory, expectorant and skin tonic. It was used to treat measles, cough, sprains, and scabies.

The tuber is aromatic, stimulant and a tonic. It is also useful in curing periodic attacks of hysteria and convulsions. Its juice or dry powder, mixed in buttermilk or plain water, is highly beneficial in intestinal problems, especially chronic diarrhoea. About 20 drops of juice of raw turmeric, mixed with a pinch of salt, taken first thing in the morning is considered an effective remedy for expelling worms.

Early Sanskrit works mentioned turmeric. Both Ayurvedic and Unani practitioners were familiar with its medicinal properties. It was administered to strengthen the working of the stomach. It was mixed with honey to treat anemia. For measles, dry turmeric roots were powdered and mixed with a few drops of honey along with the juice of few bitter gourd leaves. It was also an effective remedy for chronic cough and throat irritations. Half a teaspoon of fresh turmeric powder mixed in warm milk worked wonders for bronchial asthma. Turmeric with caraway seeds or *ajwain* helped tackle stubborn colds. It's paste mixed with lime and salt was used to treat sprains. Your grandmother knew this, before western laboratories discovered it.

Now, western labs are agog with it. In just one year of 2004, as many as 256 papers on turmeric were published in the United States. At the moment there are clinical trials going on in the US to study curcumin treatment for various ailments like cancer, Alzheimer's and multiple myeloma. Studies have shown a low incidence of colorectal cancer among groups that consumed turmeric suggesting that it may have anti-cancer properties.

Turmeric is also used in the production of sunscreens. In India, it is a common practice to smear turmeric paste on the outer skin of a bride, as it is believed to be a good cosmetic giving a glow to the skin and destroying bacteria.

The government of Thailand is funding a project to ascertain whether they can identify some compounds in turmeric that can be used in cosmetics.

With new western research showing what the yellow magical powder can do for health, it is soon destined to add colour to western cuisine. But India's traditional knowledge still does not get the respect it deserves.

□□

HOW TO SELECT AND STORE

Even though dried herbs and spices are widely available in matter, explore the local spice stores or ethnic markets in your area. Oftentimes, these stores feature an expansive selection of dried herbs and spices that are of superior quality and freshness than those offered in regular markets. Just like with other dried spices, try to select organically grown turmeric since this will give you more assurance that the herb has not been irradiated. Since the colour of turmeric varies among varieties, it is not a criterion of quality.

For the most curcumin, be sure to use turmeric rather curry powder—a study analyzing curcumin content in 28 spice products described as turmeric or curry powders found that pure turmeric powder had the highest concentration of curcumin, averaging 3.14% by weight. The curry powder samples, with one exception, contained very small amounts of curcumin.

Turmeric powder should kept in a tightly sealed container in a cool, dark and dry place. Fresh turmeric rhizome should be kept in the refrigerator.

Tips for Preparing Turmeric

Be careful when using turmeric since its deep colour can easily stain. To avoid a lasting stain, quickly wash any area with which it has made contact with soap and water. To prevent staining your hands, you might consider wearing kitchen gloves while handling turmeric.

If you are able to find turmeric rhizomes in the grocery store, you can make your own fresh turmeric powder by boiling, drying and then grinding it into a fine consistency.

□□

HEALING PROPERTIES OF TURMERIC

Besides flavouring food, to purify the blood and skin conditions remedy is probably the most common use of turmeric in Ayurveda.

❑ The main organs that turmeric treats are the skin, heart, liver and lungs.

❑ Turmeric is used for epilepsy and bleeding disorders, skin diseases, to purify the body-mind, and to help the lungs expel *kapha*.

❑ **Activities of Turmeric include:** Alterative, analgesic, antibacterial, anti-inflammatory, anti-tumor, anti-allergic, antioxidant, antiseptic, antispasmodic, appetizer, astringent, cardiovascular, carminative, cholagogue, digestive, diuretic, stimulant, and vulnerary.

❑ **Therapeutic uses of Turmeric:** Anemia, cancer, diabetes, digestion, food poisoning, gallstones, indigestion, parasites, poor circulation, staph infections, and wounds.

❏ Turmeric helps to regulate the female reproductive system and purifies the uterus and breast milk, and in men it purifies and builds semen, which is counterintuitive for a pungent bitter.

❏ Turmeric reduces fevers, diarrhoea, urinary disorders, insanity, poisoning, cough, and lactation problems in general.

❏ Turmeric is used to treat external ulcers that respond to nothing else. Turmeric decreases *kapha* and so is used to remove mucus in the throat, watery discharges like leucorrhoea, and any pus in the eyes, ears, or in wounds, etc.

❏ In Ayurvedic cooking, turmeric is everywhere, this multifaceted wonder spice helps

- Detoxify the liver
- Balance cholesterol levels
- Fight allergies
- Stimulate digestion
- Boost immunity
- Enhance the complexion

It is also an antioxidant Ayurveda recognizes turmeric as a heating spice, contributing bitter, pungent and astringent tastes.

In general turmeric is used for

- Weak stomachs
- Poor digestion
- Dyspepsia
- To normalize metabolism
- To help digest protein
- To increase the bio-availability of food and the ability of the stomach to withstand digestive acids.

Turmeric is a great carminative, able to calm an upset digestive system by getting rid of gas and distention.

16   *Turmeric—1*

Carminatives also tend to increase absorption and nurture the intestinal flora.

Taking turmeric will work fine to balance an upset digestion. Just take a small spoonful of turmeric and stir it in a cup of yogurt right after lunch.

Remedy for 'piles' is to directly apply a mixture of mustard oil, turmeric, and onion juice. To stop rectal bleeding take a 2 or 3 tablespoons of turmeric every half hour until the bleeding stops, usually in an hour.

▭▭

HEALTH BENEFITS OF TURMERIC

There are many health benefits of turmeric. These benefits also come from curcumin, which is an ingredient in turmeric. Turmeric is the spice from India that is used in curry dishes. Curcumin is the part of turmeric that gives curry food its golden colour. This also provides turmeric with curcuminoids, which are believed to have health properties such as antioxidant, antibacterial and anti-inflammatory qualities.

Turmeric benefits have been known for centuries and have always been an important part of Chinese herbal medicine and also the Ayurvedic medicine of India. This natural food is believed to support liver health, help prevent bad cholesterol, and it is being studied for its ability to block tumors.

In laboratory studies at the University of Texas, preliminary research found turmeric to be useful in preventing and blocking the growth of cancer such as melanoma tumor cells, breast cancer, colon cancer and other cancers.

Some researchers believe there also appears to be some kind of association between reduced rates of leukemia and colon cancer, and populations of countries that consume a diet with higher amounts of curcumin from turmeric.

These findings are promising but are not proof of cures. Further studies are needed of course. But the preliminary research is exciting and promising for the relationship between turmeric and the possible help in prevention of various cancers.

Many other reputed health benefits of turmeric extract include a reputation for supporting healthy skin care, healthy cholesterol levels, liver and gall-bladder health and possible joint pain relief through anti-inflammatory and antioxidant properties.

The antioxidant power of turmeric is so effective that it actually helps preserve the shelf life of foods that it is added to. In the following lines, we have mentioned the health benefits arising from the use of turmeric.

❒ Turmeric has antiseptic properties. Putting its powder over cuts, bruises, or scrapes helps in stopping blood loss as well as healing the wounds.

❒ Drinking boiled milk, with a little turmeric powder in it, helps in the strengthening of bones.

❒ The anti-inflammatory properties of turmeric powder help in alleviating the pain associated with arthritis and rheumatoid arthritis.

❒ Taking turmeric on a regular basis helps in the reduction of fats, thus aiding in weight loss.

❒ Turmeric powder, when consumed regularly, helps improve blood circulation and also purifies blood.

❒ Studies have shown that turmeric helps in prevention and blockage of the growth of melanoma tumor cells, breast cancer, colon cancer and other cancers.

❒ Turmeric extract is believed to cure liver problems as well as prevent bad cholesterol.

❒ Turmeric has been said to help reduce the risk of childhood leukemia.

- Turmeric powder aids the healing process and remodelling of damaged skin.

- Turmeric has been known to be helpful in treating psoriasis and other inflammatory skin conditions.

- Turmeric is said to be very good for digestion.

- Turmeric powder, when mixed with cucumber lemon or juice, helps in the reduction of pigmentation.

- Paste of turmeric and milk cream or turmeric and curd, when applied on stomach, helps in lightening of stretch marks.

- Applying a paste of turmeric, gram flour and milk cream is believed to help in giving a glow to the skin.

⊓⊓

MULTI-PURPOSE TURMERIC

Turmeric is a spice widely used in India in cooking various curries. It has also been used since ancient times as a traditional medicine and also for beauty care. In the Ayurveda system of Indian medicine, it is an important herbal medicine prescribed for various ailments. It is very commonly used throughout India as an ingredient for traditional beauty care treatments.

The Ayurveda is an ancient Sanskrit text of Indian medicine which describes the use of various herbs and also other remedies of traditional medicine like incantations and amulets for a whole range of ailments and also beauty care. Turmeric is considered as an important part of the range of herbal medicines described in this text.

Turmeric is used in Ayurveda in two ways— freshly extracted turmeric juice, which is taken orally, and turmeric paste used for skin application.

Raw turmeric is actually a rhizome of curcuma longa similar to ginger in appearance. This raw vegetable is crushed and the strained extracted juice forms a translucent reddish-yellow liquid which is more or less tasteless. These juice is then to be taken either raw or if the person wishes, mixed with honey preferably early in the morning on empty stomach. A wide range of benefit is described for this treatment in the Ayurveda. The main use of turmeric juice taken regularly is as a blood purifier. In this context, it is believed to enhance health of the whole body. It is also said to be most beneficial in chronic illnesses with generalized weakness and in diseases like renal failure where toxins are released into the body. The other use of turmeric juice is in stomach ailments. It is said to have a soothing effect on the stomach and thus helps in diseases like hyperacidity and indigestion. Taken regularly, it gives a healthy glow to the skin also.

The other use of turmeric as a herbal medicine is in beauty care, where its juice is applied to the skin as a raw paste, kept for around thirty minutes and then washed off. It has been used as an herbal cosmetic in India since ancient times and is still in use even today throughout the country. It is an essential ingredient of the traditional bathing ritual of Indian marriages where it is applied along with sandal wood paste before the bath.

Regular turmeric use is said to make the skin soft and smooth. It also gives a glow to the skin and produces a fairer complexion. Turmeric is also prescribed in Indian medicine for various skin ailments where application of the paste regularly is advocated. It is used for spots of pigmentation or blotches that may appear on the skin, and also for diseases like eczema. Turmeric is also used in traditional medicine for cuts and burns as it is believed to have an antiseptic effect and also promote healing.

Besides these uses as an herbal medicine, the Ayurveda also gives some other uses of turmeric. It is said to be poisonous for crocodiles, and anyone swimming in crocodile infested waters should apply turmeric paste to protect himself! It is also believed to ward off snakes and the presence of turmeric plants around the house act as a barrier for them. The paste is also used in Indian medicine for snakebites. Its use is also advocated in various rites and spells to ward off ghosts and evil spirits.

Turmeric has also received a lot of attention in modern times from science, and its active ingredient, curcumin, has been isolated. Curcumin has been shown to have an anti-oxidant property, and is used in alternative medicine for this. It also has an anti-inflammatory effect by reducing histamine levels. It has also been shown to have a protective effect on the liver and also in atherosclerosis. These effects are still under examination through various trials, but turmeric has already become an important remedy in alternative medicine. In fact, there is even a hotly contested patent application by a US firm to control this traditional Indian medicine. Turmeric extract is now available in tablet and capsule form and can be taken orally thrice daily.

Turmeric today continues to be used very widely throughout India as an alternative medicine, and also in herbal beauty care. A modern use discovered more recently is in plugging radiator leaks! In the water cooled type of radiators, a spoonful of turmeric added to the water plugs the leak almost magically. This is just one more use of this Indian spice that continues to be reinvented and rediscovered throughout the world.

Turmeric is a unique, colourful and versatile natural plant product coumbining the properties of a spice or flavourant, colourant as brilliant yellow dye, as a cosmetic, as a source of medicine useful in a number of diseases. These virtues are discussed briefly below.

In India and other Asian countries, use of turmeric is mostly popular as food adjunct in many vegetable, meat and fish preparations. Turmeric not only adds to taste, flavour and colour of the dish but also, it is believed that it preserves the food. Moreover, due to its medicinal virtues, by consuming turmeric regularly with food in any form, it prevents many diseases. Turmeric, by dint of its aromatic oil content, flavours foodstuffs, acts as an appetiser and adds digestion.

It is also used to colour liquor, fruit drinks, cakes and table jellies. It is used to flavour and at the same time colour butter, cheese, margarine, pickles, mustard and other foodstuffs.

Before use of chemical dye was introduced, turmeric was commonly used in India for dyeing wool, silk and 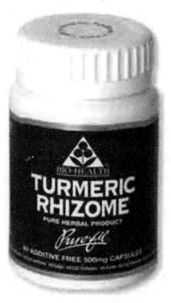 cotton to impart yellow shade, in an acid bath. It is still used for dyeing cotton. The use of natural dye is now being encouraged due to craze created in global market. However, yellow dye from turmeric has one major lacuna. Though there is washing fastness, it lacks in light fastness. The dye is also employed as coloring material in pharmacy, confectionery, rice milling and food industry. Considerable quantities of turmeric are converted as *Kumkum* used in *Tilak*. A diluted tincture of turmeric is suitable for use as a fluorescence indicator even in brown and yellow solutions.

Turmeric has been traditionally regarded as important source of medicine. It is said to be anti-oxidant, due to the phenolic character of curcuma. It is considered useful both for internal and external applications. It is considered useful for cancer patients. It is a stomachic, carminative, tonic, blood purifier, vermicide, and an antiseptic. It is taken with warm milk to act as expectorant. Mixed with lime it is applied externally to get relief from sprains and pains. It is used as an inhalation from boiling water or smoked through pipe to get relief from sore throat and congestion.

In chicken pox, it is applied as paste with gingerly oil and neem leaves. The juice of raw rhizome is used an anti-parasitic for many skin affections. Burnt turmeric is used as tooth powder to relieve dental troubles.

Turmeric is considered as excellent natural cosmetics. Smearing turmeric paste on the face and limbs during the bath is found to clear the skin and beautify the face. Many cosmetics are now available in the market manufactured using turmeric as one of the ingredients.

Turmeric has been used worldwide since very ancient times. Several unique properties of the Indian turmeric make it an ideal choice as a food flavour. It also finds use in the preparation of liquors, dyestuffs, medicines, cosmetics and toiletries. It is used as natural colourant. The curcumin present in turmeric imparts its distinctive yellow colour. In beauty care, women have used turmeric paste since very ancient times. Today it finds use as an antiseptic and an antitanning. It prevents and cures pigmentation, making skin translucent and glowing. It cools and smoothes the skin. It is used to purify blood. It also helps in protecting the skin from water allergy.

❐❐

TURMERIC AS REMEDY

You can easily named turmeric a medicinal herb. In many complications turmeric works like panacea.

Anemia

Everyday take a dose of 1 tsp of turmeric juice mixed with honey.

Asthma

Boil 1 cup of milk with 1 tsp of turmeric powder. Drink warm.

Burns

Mix 1 tsp of turmeric with 1 tsp of aloe gel and apply to burnt area.

Dental Problems

Mix 1 tsp of turmeric with ½ tsp of salt. Add mustard oil to make a paste. Rub the teeth and gums with this paste twice daily.

Conjunctivitis

Mix 1 tbsp of crushed, raw turmeric in 1/3 cup of water. Boil and sieve. 2-3 drops of this mixture may be used in each eye up to 3 times per day.

Complexion

Apply a paste of turmeric on the skin before bed, and wash off after a few minutes. In the morning, remove any remaining yellow tinge with a paste of chickpea flour (besan) and oil.

Diabetes

½-1 tsp of turmeric should be taken 3 times a day.

Diarrhoea

Take ½ tsp of turmeric powder or juice in water, 3 times per day.

Pain

☐ Mix 1 tsp of turmeric and 2 tsp of ginger with water to make a paste. Spread over a cloth, place on the affected area and bandage.

☐ Add 1 tsp of turmeric to 1 cup of warm milk and drink before bed.

Ears, Eyes, Nose and Mouth

☐ Turmeric dust, with alum 1:20, is blown into the ear to treat chronic otorrhoea.

☐ Mix a pinch of turmeric with organic ghee and apply it to the mucus lining of nose to stop the sniffles. It also stops nosebleeds, helps to clear the sinuses, restore a more acute sense of smell, and helps to purify the mind and brain.

☐ Turmeric helps to maintain the shape and integrity of our eyes.

☐ A turmeric/water decoction, 1:20, is used to treat conjunctivitis and eye disease in general. Soak a cloth in the decoction and then cover the eye with it. This helps to relieve the pain as well.

Other Uses

In cooking, turmeric acts as a yellow colouring agent. It is an important herb in Hindu rituals. It is also a ingredient in cosmetics as it is beneficial for the skin. Burning turmeric can repel insects. Inhaling the smoke can assist in coughs, asthma and congested nasal passages.

☐☐

20 HEALTH BENEFITS OF TURMERIC

Turmeric is one of nature's most powerful healers. The active ingredient in turmeric is curcumin. Turmeric has been used for over 2500 years in India, where it was most likely first used as a dye.

The medicinal properties of this spice have been slowly revealing themselves over the centuries. Long known for its anti-inflammatory properties, recent research has revealed that turmeric is a natural wonder, proving beneficial in the treatment of many different health conditions from cancer to Alzheimer's disease.

Here are 20 reasons to add turmeric to your diet :

1. It is a natural antiseptic and antibacterial agent, useful in disinfecting cuts and burns.
2. When combined with cauliflower, it has shown to prevent prostate cancer and stop the growth of existing prostate cancer.
3. Prevented breast cancer from spreading to the lungs in mice.
4. May prevent melanoma and cause existing melanoma cells to commit suicide.
5. Reduces the risk of childhood leukemia.
6. Is a natural liver detoxifier.
7. May prevent and slow the progression of Alzheimer's disease by removing amyloyd plaque buildup in the brain.
8. May prevent metastases from occurring in many different forms of cancer.

9. It is a potent natural anti-inflammatory that works as well as many anti-inflammatory drugs but without the side effects.

10. Has shown promise in slowing the progression of multiple sclerosis in mice.

11. Is a natural painkiller and cox-2 inhibitor.

12. May aid in fat metabolism and help in weight management.

13. Has long been used in Chinese medicine as a treatment for depression.

14. Because of its anti-inflammatory properties, it is a natural treatment for arthritis and rheumatoid arthritis.

15. Boosts the effects of chemo drug paclitaxel and reduces its side effects.

16. Promising studies are underway on the effects of turmeric on pancreatic cancer.

17. Studies are ongoing in the positive effects of turmeric on multiple myeloma.

18. Has been shown to stop the growth of new blood vessels in tumors.

19. Speeds up wound healing and assists in remodeling of damaged skin.

20. May help in the treatment of psoriasis and other inflammatory skin conditions.

Turmeric can be taken in powder or pill form.

Contraindications : Turmeric should not be used by people with gallstones or bile obstruction. Though turmeric is often used by pregnant women, it is important to consult with a doctor before doing so as turmeric can be a uterine stimulant.

□□

TURMERIC—THE HERBAL MEDICINE

A knife cut. Blood. Dripping incessantly. Unflustered, the Indian housewife reaches for the closest and safest remedy at hand—*Haldi*.

Bodies responding to seasonal changes with the flu, coughs, and running noses, are immediately administered with honey mixed with turmeric or turmeric mixed in milk by the homemaker, to soothe and to cure.

The Friday oil bath routines with the application of Haldi is almost sacrosanct with the South Indian women, resulting in beautiful skin, and hairless bodies. In fact, in South India, it is considered very auspicious and therefore, is the first item on the grocery list. The turmeric plant is tied around the vessel used to make Sweet pongal on the harvest festival, which is celebrated on the Makar Sankranti Day, universally celebrated on 14th of January, every year.

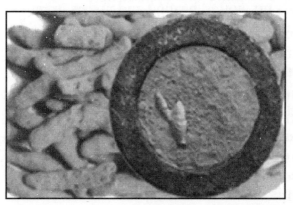

In many North Indian traditional wedding ceremonies, haldi is applied to both, the groom and the bride, not only to make them look good with fresh glowing skins, but to ward off the evil eye. It is considered by the Hindus as a symbol of prosperity and as a cleansing herb for the whole body. Pieces of crushed roots mixed with sea water are sprinkled to remove the negative influences from places, persons, and things during ceremonies.

Indians therefore, are no strangers to the multiple uses of Turmeric. It is well recognized as the best anti-oxidant, hypoglycemic, colourant, antiseptic and wound healer. Used in cooking as a spice for over 2,500 years, turmeric has a bitter, musty flavour similar to mustard. It is this spice that gives Indian curries their characteristic bright yellow-orange colour.

The healing properties of turmeric have made it a most sought after ingredient in cosmetics and drugs, as the leaf oil and extract can also be used as sunscreens and bio-pesticides.

Its modern approved applications in European medicine, stem from its traditional uses in Asia. Turmeric is used extensively in the Indian systems of medicine (Ayurveda, Unani, and Siddha). It is used as a carminative and stomachic in the treatment of digestive disorders such as flatulence, bloating, and appetite loss. Turmeric is used internally as boiled powder, fresh juice, and confection and externally as paste, oil, ointment, and lotion. It is also applied topically for ulcers, wounds, eczema, and inflammations. In both the Ayurvedic and Siddha systems of medicine, a turmeric paste is used topically to treat ulcers and scabies.

Turmeric, with its antibacterial action, prevents bacterial infections on wounds. Turmeric also has a long history of use for its anti-inflammatory and antiarthritic effects. As in India, it is used in China, Japan, and Korea for a range of indications including, Amenorrhoea. Turmeric has been investigated for its cholagogous influence on the secretion of bile, pancreatic, and gastric juices. It is currently being evaluated for its anti-carcinogenic and anti-mutagenic properties.

The roots are pounded and pressed to extract a juice that, when mixed with water, is helpful in earaches and to clear the sinuses through nasal application. The astringent qualities of turmeric are also useful in cases of consumption, tuberculosis, bronchitis, colds and asthma, the root being lightly cooked and eaten. At times, turmeric has been taken as a diuretic, and topically it can be helpful with pimples or to stop bleeding.

□□

CURATIVE TURMERIC

Turmeric is a member of the ginger family. It has been used for healing by Ayurvedic means, since time immemorial for its anti-inflammatory, antioxidant and antiseptic properties. These benefits also come from curcumin that gives curry food its golden colour. Ayurvedic practitioners state that it is a cleanser for all parts of the body as it can also be used for digestive aids, in treating infection, blood purify, arthritis, jaundice and fever.

It is believed that the herb can also cure liver health issues, prevent bad cholesterol and block tumors. A recent preliminary research states that turmeric is useful in preventing and blocking the growth of cancer such as melanoma tumor cells, breast cancer, colon cancer and other cancers. Read detailed home remedies that cures normal ailments and helps in enhancing good physical growth.

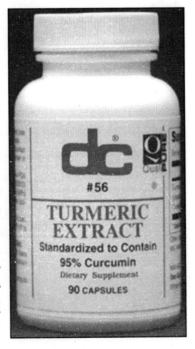

Pigmentation : Apply little turmeric mixed with cucumber juice or lemon to the affected area to reduce pigmentation. Leave on for fifteen minutes or more, and wash off. For better results do this everyday until you regain your tone colour.

Strong Bones : To strengthen bones add turmeric to the boiling milk and drink before going to bed at night. This will help in curing numerous ailments. Ayurvedic doctors, especially recommend this to women as it reduces the risk of developing osteoporosis.

Pregnancy Stretch marks : To prevent unsightly stretch marks due to pregnancy, apply a mixture of turmeric and *malai* or turmeric and curd to your stomach and waist before going for a bath. Leave it on for fifteen minutes, and wash off.

Wounds : Sprinkle a bit of turmeric with honey (optional), on cuts, bruises, or scrapes after a thorough wash, as the anti bacterial action will prevent wound infections.

Arthritis : Turmeric can also be used in reducing pain associated with arthritis. Warm a cup of milk. Before it boils, remove it from the heat and add in a teaspoon of turmeric powder in it. Stir and drink it for up to 3 times daily.

Reduce Fats : Regular use of turmeric reduces fats, aids blood circulation and purifies it.

Cosmetic Use : Make a paste of milk cream (if dry skin), gram flour and turmeric and apply it daily to your face to owe glowing skin without any marks. Make sure to scrub it well as it helps in removing black heads too.

Most of the times the turmeric packed in packets is not pure, therefore try to find the root and powder it for further use. Keep it in tightly sealed container in a cool, dark and dry place. Make sure to keep fresh turmeric rhizome in the refrigerator.

⬜⬜

TURMERIC FOR SKIN CARE

Since time immemorial, turmeric is very popular in cosmetic use especially for woman. In the East, turmeric is precious as the therapeutic goldmine inhabits significant position in the psyche of Hindu. It forms an important part of various sanctified Hindu rituals focus its importance for mankind.

In the late 1970s a scientific study on turmeric was taken up and in the beginning was restricted mostly to its anti-inflammatory characteristics. Eventually, turmeric has globally attracted for its cosmetic and therapeutic use. In the warmer parts of the world, turmeric is profitably grown. The turmeric powder has a characteristic of aroma and bitter-warm taste with orange-yellow to dark-yellow in colour.

As herb, turmeric has been used for centuries for seasoning, but through a series of complex extraction and isolation processes, it will soon be given further potential as a substance to support the medical as well as the cosmetics industries.

In the world, the biggest users of turmeric are in India. India is also major producer of turmeric. These natural plant's extracts used in cosmetic products marketed for skin care and hair care.

Skin Care and Colouring

The skin is the main portion of the body and provides a shielding barrier against harmful chemicals, microbes, and ultraviolet radiation. Natural plant products like turmeric have been formulated to heal and prevent dry skin, treat skin conditions such as eczema and acne, and retard the aging process.

Turmeric is used in many celebrations of Hindus. Especially in Hindu wedding brides would rub with turmeric on their bodies for glowing look. New born babies also rubbed with turmeric on their forehead for good luck.

Traditionally women rub turmeric on their cheeks to produce a natural golden glow, extract of turmeric has been added to creams for use as a colouring agent. A compound called curcumin is the yellow pigment in turmeric.

Washing in turmeric improves skin complexion and also reduces hair growth on body. Nowadays there are lots of herbal products in the market in which main herb used is turmeric as natural ingredient. These constitute home remedies for skin and hair problems.

Natural cleansers like milk with turmeric powder are effective natural cosmetics in themselves; it brings a healthy glow to the skin and makes them beautiful. They also help to restore or maintain youth by controlling wrinkle and crease formation on the surface of the skin. Turmeric can also benefit skin conditions including eczema, psoriasis and acne.

Effectual healing properties of turmeric have made it accepted after ingredient in cosmetics and drugs, as the leaf oil of turmeric and extract can also be used as bio-pesticides and sunscreens.

In addition to colour and flavour into many oriental cuisines, turmeric powder is valuable for its aromatic, stimulatory and carminative properties as well as for curing

many ailments both minor such as sore throat and coryza as well as major afflictions. It is eminent for accelerated healing of both septic and non-septic wounds.

Turmeric is also very effective tonic and a blood purifier. It is also skin-friendly and constitutes an important ingredient of many creams and lotions.

Hair Care

For the treatment of dandruff, and as hair colorants and dyes, plant extracts are used as hair growth stimulators, the mechanism of action appears to be an acceleration of blood circulation or increased nutrition to the hair follicles.

Natural dyes derived from plant extracts are being used in hair colorant products; curcumin from turmeric also used in natural dye produces a range of colour from yellow to deep orange.

Skin Disease

A fresh juice from rhizome or (the aboveground and underground roots) a paste prepared from turmeric or decoction is often used as a local application as well as internally in the treatment of leprosy skin disease.

In case of chickenpox, turmeric is applied as a powder or as a paste to facilitate the process of scabbing.

◻◻

HOW CAN YOU GET THE MAXIMUM BENEFITS

In order to get the maximum turmeric benefits, you have to make sure you are taking a supplement with standardized herbal extract of pure turmeric. Many turmeric products on the market do not use standardized extract, because it is much cheaper to produce. But beware, because these products do not contain enough active ingredient to offer you turmeric benefits.

Also, you must make sure that the turmeric product is manufactured at a facility that follows strict GMP compliance. These are the strictest manufacturing standards in the world—the same standards that pharmaceutical drugs have to follow—so you know that they are the highest quality products you can buy.

It is important to note that herbal products are considered dietary supplements, so manufacturers do not have to guarantee the content or effectiveness of their products.

As a result many of these products contain very little or none of the ingredients they claim to (therefore, no benefits) or too much ingredient (dangerous!). Still others contain harmful contaminants that could cause serious damage to your body.

That's why you have to find a high quality turmeric supplement, one with standardized herbal extract.

Are you better off with turmeric on its own or as part of a more comprehensive formula?

You can purchase an individual turmeric supplement, or you can buy a more comprehensive product that includes turmeric extract along with other herbs, vitamins and minerals. In our opinion, you are better off with the latter for many reasons.

Maximize the Turmeric Extract Benefits

Many herbalists and scientists feel that you can achieve better results with a blend of herbs, vitamins, minerals and other nutrients in one formula. Here's why:

❏ Many herbs, vitamins, minerals and other nutrients work together synergistically—often a blend of nutrients can work better together than one nutrient on its own. The therapeutic effect is enhanced by the nutrients working together.

For example : Turmeric can work together with green tea and olive leaf to lower cholesterol. Vitamin E works in conjunction with Vitamin-C in a similar fashion.

❏ You can help several body systems at one time—For example, you can treat a condition with one herb, protect your body with another and make sure the condition does not return with yet another herb.

For example, Turmeric can improve blood flow while Vitamin E can strengthen your heart and maintains the circulatory system.

❏ Herbs can offset the possible side effects of each other —an herb that helps alleviate a problem in one area can help treat a slight side effect that may be caused by another.

For example : Turmeric could cause a mild side effect that is easily treated with ginger present in the product.

So, it is very important to find a high quality product.

❏❏

TRADITIONAL USES OF TURMERIC

Since ancient times, turmeric has been used as a traditional medicine and for beauty care. In Ayurvedic system of Indian medicine, turmeric is an important herbal medicine prescribed for various diseases.

The various uses of turmeric are as follows :

Food Additive

❐ Turmeric is a mild aromatic stimulant used in in the manufacture of curry powders.

❐ Turmeric is used in products that are packaged to protect them from sunlight.

❐ The oleoresin component of turmeric is used for oil-containing products.

❐ The curcumin solution or curcumin powder dissolved in alcohol is used for water containing products.

❐ Sometimes in pickles and mustard, turmeric is used to compensate for fading.

❐ Turmeric is also used for colouring cheeses, salad dressings, margarine, yoghurts, cakes, biscuits, popcorn, cereals, sauces, etc.

❐ Turmeric also forms a substitute for mustard in the cattle feed.

Medicinal

❐ Turmeric is used for treating digestive disorders.

❐ Raw turmeric juice is used to treat hyper acidity and indigestion.

- The juice of raw turmeric also acts as a blood purifier.
- Curcumin—an active component of turmeric, has anti-oxidant properties and so turmeric is used in alternative medicine.
- Turmeric is used for cuts and burns as it is believed to have antiseptic effects and promotes healing.

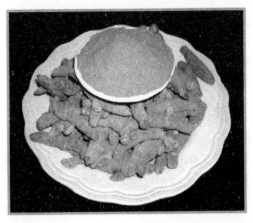

- Curcumin also has an anti-inflammatory effect by reducing histamine (hormone) levels.
- The flouride present in turmeric is essential for teeth.
- Turmeric also has a protective effect on the liver and also in atherosclerosis.

Cosmetics

- The juice of raw turmeric is applied to the skin as a paste, kept for around thirty minutes and then washed off. It adds glow to the skin.
- It is an essential ingredient of the traditional bathing ritual of Indian marriages where it is applied along with sandal wood paste before the bath.
- It is believed that regular bathing in water containing turmeric reduces growth of body hair.
- Regular turmeric use is said to make the skin fair, soft and smooth.

❐ Turmeric is used for spots caused due to pigmentation or blotches and also for diseases like eczema.

As a tester for Acids and Alkalies

Unglazed white paper is saturated with an alcoholic solution of curcumin. When dried, this paper is used for testing of alkalies, acids and boric acid.

❐ **Alkali and Acid Test :** The paper turns red-brown with alkalies. This colour becomes violet upon drying and the original yellow colour is restored with acids.

❐ **Boric Acid Test :** When the paper is dipped into a solution of boric acid, it turns orange-red. The colour remains so even when it is moistened with free mineral acid. Paper that has been turned to orange by boric acid will assume a blue colour when it is moistened with diluted alkali.

Miscellaneous Uses

❐ Ayurveda states that turmeric is poisonous for crocodiles. So anyone swimming in crocodile infested waters should apply turmeric paste to protect himself.

❐ Turmeric is also believed to ward off snakes and the presence of turmeric plants around the house acts as a barrier for them.

❐ The turmeric paste is used in Indian medicine for snakebites.

❐ The leaves of turmeric are said to act as mosquito repellents.

❐ Turmeric is used as a colouring agent for filter paper used in scientific tests.

❐ It has been recently discovered that in water cooled type of radiators, a spoonful of turmeric added to the water, plugs any leaks.

❐❐

CURATIVE PROPERTIES OF TURMERIC

Turmeric is stringent and sour in taste. It is a time-tested beauty aid and a nourishing herb which not only gives natural gloss, royal glow and lustre but also imparts vigour and youthful vitality to the entire body. Turmeric is thus a great tonic in general, aromatic, diuretic, expectorant, blood-purifier, skin-tonic, carminative, pain reliever, germicidal, anti-flatulent, producer and enhancer of red blood corpuscles, anti-phlegm, antibilleous, protector of eyes, anti-inflammatory and imparts coolness to the system.

Bruises, Sprain and Wounds

☐ Applying paste of turmeric powder with lime or water on the effected part eliminates swelling and pain in bruises.

☐ Taking 1 tsp. turmeric powder with hot milk is also useful.

☐ Filling the wound or cut, (from which blood is oozing) with Turmeric powder will stop bleeding and curing of the wound/cut.

☐ Applying poultice made of gram flour, turmeric powder mixed with mustard or til oil on the sprained portion enhances blood circulation and gives relief.

☐ Tying a bandage of turmeric (prepared with 4 tsp. flour, 2 tsp. turmeric powder, 1 tsp. pure ghee, ½ tsp. sendha salt with water) on the bruised portion gives relief.

- Giving fomentation with cloth soaked in hot water (500 gm. water boiled with 1 tsp. sendha salt and 1 tsp. turmeric powder) on the bruised part eliminates pain and swelling.

- Giving fomentation with potli (having one ground onion mixed with 1 tsp. turmeric powder) heated with resame oil on the bruised portion gives relief.

- Applying turmeric powder heated in ghee or oil on the wound and tying it with a bandage helps in quick healing.

- Dusting turmeric powder on wounds also helps.

Skin-problems

- **Ringworm White spots** : Applying paste of turmeric rubbed on stone with water on the affected portion is useful.

- **Skin eruptions** : Applying paste of turmeric and resame oil on the body prevents skin eruptions.

- Applying turmeric powder or paste on the body before bath is a preventive against skin problems and also a depilatory. (clears the growth of hair on body).

- **Urticaria** : Taking 1 tsp. turmeric powder with 1 tsp. honey twice a day cures Urticaria.

- Taking halwa (made from 2 tsp. flour, 1 tsp. ghee, 1 tsp. turmeric, 2 tsp. sugar, 1 cup water) in the morning cures Utricaria.

- Taking roasted turmeric with gur cures itching.

- **Eczema** : Sucking tablet of ground turmeric with honey for 10-15 days cures Eczema.

- **Pustules** : Placing cotton dipped in turmeric oil over pustules gives relief.

- **Freckles, spots** : Applying turmeric rubbed on stone with water eliminates them.

- Massaging the face with ubtan (mix ground turmeric

with milk of banyan or pipal and soak it overnight) 1 hour before bath eliminates freckles on the face and imparts natural glow.

Cough & Cold, Asthma

☐ Taking turmeric powder and little salt with hot water or sucking a small piece of turmeric or licking.

1 tsp. turmeric powder with ¼ tsp. honey gives relief in cough and eliminates congestion of bronchi.

☐ Taking ¼ tsp. turmeric with hot milk is helpful in checking running nose.

☐ Inhaling the smoke of burnt turmeric throws out the trapped phlegm.

☐ Taking ¼ tsp. powder of turmeric (roasted in hot sand and then ground) with hot water relieves breathing problem.

☐ Taking turmeric boiled in milk and sweetened with jaggery is very useful in cold and asthma.

☐ Sucking a piece of turmeric (like lemon drops) or keeping it in mouth at night cures chronic cold.

☐ Licking tablets (made by mixing turmeric powder, barley powder and bansa-ash in equal proportion with honey and making small tablets) 4-5 times in a day eliminates trapped phlegm in the body.

☐ Massaging the throat and chest with little Turmeric-powder, ground black pepper mixed with ghee cures irritation in bronchial chords.

☐ Giving a pinch of turmeric powder with milk to children gives quick relief.

☐ Inhaling smoke of cow-dung cake with turmeric sprinkled on it releases the trapped phlegm.

☐ Taking ¼ tsp. of turmeric powder with 3-4 gulps of warm water acts as a preventive against attack of asthma.

Whooping Cough

☐ Taking 1 tsp. ground roasted turmeric powder with two spoons of honey 3 or 4 times a day gives relief in cough.

☐ Taking betel with little turmeric piece is also useful.

Indigestion & Stomach Problems

☐ Taking turmeric powder and salt in equal quantity with warm water gives instant relief in acidity.

☐ Taking 1 tsp. churna (grind turmeric 4 gms., sonth 4 gms., black pepper 2 gms. and cardamom 2 gms.) after meals is digestive, eliminates wind and stomach ailments.

☐ Taking curd or whey with turmeric powder after lunch cures digestive problems.

☐ Licking Turmeric powder mixed with honey 2-3 times a day cures soreness.

Tonsilitis

Fomentation with paste made of 10 gms. turmeric powder roasted in mustard oil and then tied around the neck gives relief in tonsils.

Blisters in Mouth

Gargling with a glass water in which little turmeric powder is boiled, twice a day, cures it.

Urinary Troubles

Taking paste of ground or juice of raw turmeric and honey with goat's milk (if available) twice a day, cures all urinary problems.

Chicken-pox

☐ Taking 1 tsp. powder of turmeric and imli (tamarind) for 4-5 days acts as a preventive against it.

☐ Applying a thin layer of the ubtan (turmeric powder, foam of fresh milk and wheat flour mixed with mustard oil or fresh cream) on the affected part twice a day flattens the deep spots of chicken-pox and makes the skin soft.

Worms

Licking the paste (made of ¼ tsp. turmeric powder and ½ tsp. Vayavidang Churna with 1 tsp. of honey for 7-8 days kills worms and throws them out.

Pregnancy and Postnatal Care

☐ Taking 5-10 gms. of turmeric powder with water during menses is an anti-pregnancy dose for ladies.

☐ Taking 1 tsp turmeric powder with hot milk in latter part of the 9th month of pregnancy helps in easy delivery.

☐ Taking 1 tsp. roasted turmeric powder with gur after delivery eliminates weakness and cures uterus swelling.

Pain in Breasts

Applying paste of turmeric rubbed on stone on the affected part eliminates pain.

Gout

Taking laddu of turmeric (mix ½ kg. roasted ground turmeric, one finely grated dried coconut, 1 kg. jaggery, 200 gm. cashew nuts or ground nuts and make laddus) daily in the morning with basil or lemon tea makes the joints supple and gives relief in pain and swelling.

Pain in Ribs

Applying paste of turmeric powder mixed in hot water on the aching ribs gives relief or massaging the ribs with turmeric oil or massaging the ribs with paste of turmeric powder in milk of the aak plant gives quick relief.

Jaundice & Liver Problems

Taking 4-5 gms. of turmeric powder mixed in a glass of whey twice a day activates the liver.

Diabetes

Taking 4-5 gms. ground turmeric with water or honey twice a day is helpful in curing diabetes.

Leucorrhoea

☐ Taking Turmeric powder with sugar twice a day for sometime checks this.

☐ Washing the private parts with turmeric water (10 gms. turmeric boiled in 100 ml. water) is also useful. Alongwith it taking one batasha with 8-10 drops of milk of banyan tree before sunrise for 7 days helps in early cure.

Debility in Males

Taking about 7-8 gms. of raw ground turmeric and equal amount of honey with goat's milk cures debillty in males.

Dental Problems

☐ Rinsing the mouth with turmeric water (boil 5 gms. turmeric powder, 2 cloves and 2 dried leaves of guava in 200 gms. water) gives instant relief.

☐ Applying and rubbing the teeth with paste of turmeric powder, salt and mustard oil strengthens the gums.

☐ Massaging the aching teeth with roasted ground turmeric eliminate pain and swelling.

☐ Keeping piece of roasted turmeric near the aching tooth and letting the saliva ooze out also helps.

☐ Filling the cavity in teeth with roasted ground turmeric powder gives relief from pain.

☐ Applying the powder of burnt turmeric piece and

ajwain on teeth and cleaning them makes the gums and teeth strong.

Ear Troubles

Putting one or two drops of turmeric (by roasting 2 pieces of turmeric in mustard oil) in the ear, cleaning it with an ear-bud cures ear-problems.

Eye Troubles

☐ Cloth dipped in the solution of turmeric powder and water is employed as an eye-shade.

☐ Dropping turmeric water (1 tsp. turmeric powder boiled in 500 ml. water till 125 ml. water is left. Cool and strain it through a fine cloth) in the eyes twice a day and putting the cotton soaked in water on the eyelids relieves pain, redness, irritation and itching in the eyes.

☐ Applying, bit heated paste of piece of turmeric rubbed on stone on eyelids also eliminates pain, swelling and eye-troubles.

☐ A decoction of turmeric powder with water as a cooling lotion on the eyes is useful in conjunctivites.

Poison of Insect-bite

Applying the mixture of Turmeric powder and lime over the affected part nullifies the toxic effect.

Coryza

Inhalations of fumes of burning turmeric passed into the nostrils relieves coryza.

☐☐

USES OF TURMERIC IN AUSPICIOUS OCASSIONS

Simultaneously with mehendi the ritual of haldi is also done in India. It is called the haldi ceremony where a day before the wedding, haldi paste is applied to the bride by her female relatives and friends. In many castes it is celebrated together with the mehendi ceremony and in some caste it is celebrated a day before the wedding in that case the mehendi ceremony is held a couple of day before the marriage. The haldi ceremony is held in both bride and groom's place. In the groom's house female relatives of the groom apply haldi on him and douse him with water.

Haldi ceremony is a major part of the Indian wedding ceremony and is also marked by several customs as well

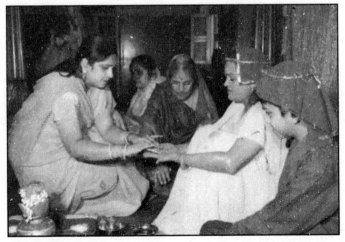

as traditions. India is a colourful nation and most of the celebrations in India are colourful too. In India, people celebrate so many festivals and ceremonies in their own ways by following their own traditions and rituals. Haldi ceremony is one of the interesting rituals of an Indian wedding.

On the day of haldi ceremony, traditionally an Indian bride has to wear yellow coloured clothes (any colour except white and black). In India, the haldi ceremony is also known as *Ubtan*. Traditionally, this ceremony of haldi is followed in each and every marriage ceremony, so that the bride can have sparkling skin on the bright day of marriage. Moreover, it is a very interesting as well as fun filled ceremony where everybody actively takes equal part.

Turmeric in Indonesia

Being its roots in Indonesia turmeric or *kunyit* in Indonesian, is used as an important spice in many countries around Asia where rice is the staple.

Turmeric gives dishes a musky flavour and a yellow colour. It has been used for centuries in Indonesia, not only in the culinary sense, but also in traditional medicine.

At special events, turmeric yellow, or *kuning emas,* is often used to colour certain items. The colour is obtained by grating and pressing a fresh turmeric rhizome.

During the period of Dutch administration, some important regional heads, called bupati, were given distinctive rewards for their loyalty to the Dutch Government. These rewards were dark green and turmeric coloured cotton parasols and gave the holder the right to VIP treatment.

At certain regional wedding ceremonies, turmeric is used to colour raw rice grains, which are later tossed toward the bridegroom when he enters the house of his spouse-to-be.

The rice is also mixed with coins, causing female guests to rush to collect as many as they can. Many believe if they collect some coins and yellow rice, wedding bells will also soon be ringing for them.

At many wedding ceremonies, the main dish is *nasi kuning*—a turmeric yellow-coloured rice dish served to the bride and bridegroom for their first marital meal together.

Turmeric blends easily with many spices. It can even be used in the same spice mix as coriander, cumin, *galangal* and pepper.

Ingredients such as *salam* leaves, lemon grass and chilies are perhaps the most suitable turmeric companions. Mixing coconut milk with turmeric will give a dish an attractive golden accent.

For a refreshing and medicinal Javanese brew for the ladies, they just peel and slice about 15 grams of fresh turmeric rhizome, put it in a pot, add 400-500 milliliters of water, 2 teaspoons of tamarind paste, some brown sugar to taste and bring to the boil for 3-4 minutes.

Lower flame and continue simmering until a herbal aroma is obvious. Let cool and take a sip to check taste. Drinking 100 milliliters of this drink, known as *kunyit asam*, twice a day can relieve cramps, especially during premenstrual periods.

□□

HALDI KUMKUM

The traditional kumkum is made from dried turmeric. The turmeric is dried and powdered with a lime/lemon giving the rich red coloured kumkum or Roli. Kumkum is used as a *Tilak*.

Kumkum, which is made from the turmeric powder is an auspicious symbol. Kumkum is applied to the forehead of a visiting girl or married woman as a sign of blessing and respect. However, it is not offered to widows. Men wear the mystic central kumkum dot as a mark of spiritual intelligence and also during religious ceremonies.

In the ancient Puranas the practice of using kumkum on the forehead has been mentioned.

According to ancient beliefs, the sixth chakra called *Ajna* is present in the area between the eyebrows. This chakra is said to be the seat of concealed wisdom, command and concentration. During meditation, the latent energy (*Kundalini*) rises from the base of the spine towards the head. This *Ajna Chakra* is the probable outlet for this strong energy. The red kumkum between the eyebrows is said to retain energy in the human body and control the various levels of concentration.

Kumkum represents intellect and is a symbol of auspiciousness and happiness in the family. It also denotes *Soubhagya* (good fortune) when used by Indian women denoting that their husbands are alive. A widow never wears kumkum. Kumkum is also not worn during mourning.

□□

RICHNESS OF TURMERIC

The scientific name of turmeric is *Curcuma longa*. The turmeric powder is prepared by the roots of this plant. These roots are hard and brittle. When tender, the outer skin of these roots has dark brown or yellowish green colour, the inside of the roots has orange mixed brown or bright red colour. The roots are cleaned, boiled, dried and then powdered to get the 'turmeric powder'. The powder prepared in this way has yellow colour and very good aroma.

Auspicious uses of Turmeric: Turmeric has the first place in any *pooja*, wedding, thread ceremony, house-warming ceremony etc. Any *pooja* starts with turmeric and kumkum particularly in South India. Turmeric is mixed with water, given a shape of dome and worshiped as Goddess Gauri. In *poojas*, usually people wear the cloths soaked in turmeric (and then dried).

Turmeric in Kitchen: Turmeric is the most important ingredient in Indian dishes. It gives colour, taste and aroma to the dishes. This has blood purifying, antiseptic and digestive properties. In recent days, we are seeing an increase in usage of artificial food ingredients in various food and food products, which may affect our health adversely. With the intake of turmeric, the adverse effects on health can be controlled.

Turmeric in Cosmetics: Turmeric is a very safe and effective beauty product.

❐ Apply a paste of turmeric and sandal wood paste to face and wash it after 10 minutes. This helps in making the face glow and cures pimples.

- Tender turmeric root and Raktachandan are mixed with milk and applied to face twice in a day. This makes the face glow.

- Turmeric root mixed in coconut milk helps in getting rid of pimples and makes the skin more healthy and soft.

- Mix turmeric powder, *besan* and fenugreek powder in equal quantities with milk, apply this to body and take bath. This removes unwanted hair from the body and makes the skin soft and beautiful.

Turmeric as Medicine: Turmeric is full of medicinal values.

- Turmeric has anti-cancer properties.

- For cold and throat pain, mix 2 teaspoons turmeric with 1-cup warm water and drink. (*We usually drink turmeric and pepper mixed with hot milk whenever we get throat pain or cough. This gives immediate relief*).

- For the cuts from sharp knifes, turmeric is applied to the cut and pressed to stop the bleeding.

- Mix clean turmeric powder with coconut oil, apply to body and take bath after sometime, to reduce the occurrences of skin diseases.

- Mix turmeric powder, ginger, garlic with milk and keep it for boiling. Drink this milk before going to bed to overcome cold and throat pain.

- The intake of turmeric keeps a pregnant woman healthy. This helps to increase the antibiotic properties in babies.

- For cough, drink 1-teaspoon turmeric mixed with 1-teaspoon honey. Followed by this, drink hot milk.

- Mix turmeric and *amla* in equal quantities with 1-tea spoon hot water and drink twice daily. This helps in controlling diabetes.

- ❏ Applying turmeric to boils in mouth helps to overcome the boils.
- ❏ Turmeric is good for people with heart problems.
- ❏ Mix turmeric with buttermilk and drink to overcome jaundice, piles.
- ❏ Mix turmeric with salt, brush teeth with this mixture to reduce tooth pain.
- ❏ Intake of tender turmeric mixed with pepper is good for urine problems.
- ❏ Mix turmeric with milk cream and apply to dry lips, hands and legs.

❏❏

TURMERIC—THE GOLDEN GODDESS

In Durga temples a mixture of turmeric and lime is commonly used. In Kali worship the gurusi is practiced using turmeric water mixed with lime, which gives a deep red colour similar to blood. The turmeric lime water mix is daily used in most Kali/Durga temples, in daily worship.

The worship of Gauri in northen India begins with Ganesh Chaturthi fast beginning from the fourth day of Bhadra (Aug-Sept). The worship begins with the drawing of the traditional diagram in front of every household using turmeric powder and dying the sacred thread with turmeric or saffron. It was a common practice both among the Aryans and the Dravidians to mark their forehead with Kumkum using saffron, where as the Dravidians used turmeric powder mixed with chalk or lime.

There is a school of thought who thinks that the auspicious or sacred association attributed to turmeric is the direct outcome of sun worship in one from or other. The idea of festivity connected with the colour yellow, through its association with the Sun, has given turmeric an erotic significance. This is another reson why it is the chief colour at weddings. Apart from the custom of smearing the body with turmeric at weddings, garments dyed or marking at the corners with turmeric colour are considered lucky and possess protective powers.

Turmeric is mentioned in Ramayana as one of the eight ingredients of *Arghya*, a respectful oblation made to gods and venerable men. All the religious customary practices in the temples are associated with turmeric and turmeric powder in which often the participants are smeared with turmeric paste all over the body. If any wound occurs as a part of the ritual, there also only turmeric powder is used for healing.

Snake worship is prevalent among all tribal communicaties in India, which still survive in many societies. Turmeric powder is used in snake worship (*Nagapooja*) from ancient days. This practice of offering turmeric powder is prevalent in all temples of goddess Durga.

In many Indian villages in older days there were people practicing sorcery, who were also assumed the role of physicians and they dispelled the diseases by transferring it to similar coloured substances. Turmeric was applied over the body of patient suffering from jaundice and the sorcerer carried out the magical expulsion of the disease. After that the turmeric was washed off together with the turmeric.

World widely, turmeric is used as spice to add colour and flavour to food. In our country almost all the recipes include turmeric as an inevitable ingredient. We consider it not merely as a protective substance, which helps in eliminating the noxious components if any in the dishes that are cooked.

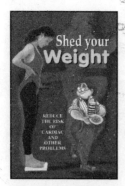

Set of
Small Size
ENGLISH
GENERAL BOOKS

☐ Home Gardening	50.00
☐ 101 Feng Shui Tips	50.00
☐ 101 Vastu Tips	50.00
☐ Dadi Maa's Home Remedies	50.00
☐ Pregnancy & Child Care	40.00
☐ Baby Health & Child Care	40.00
☐ All About Yoga	40.00
☐ Diabetes Cause & Cure	40.00
☐ Hypertension Cause & Cure	40.00
☐ Shed Your Weight	40.00
☐ How to Increase Your Height	40.00
☐ How to Increase Sex Power	40.00

SET OF SMALL ENGLISH JOKE BOOKS

☐ Juicy Joke Book (Surendra Mohan Pathak)	50.00
☐ Midnight Jokes	30.00
☐ Party Jokes	30.00
☐ Naughty Jokes	30.00
☐ Spicy Jokes	30.00
☐ Tickling Jokes	30.00
☐ Superhit Jokes	30.00
☐ Non-Veg Jokes	30.00
☐ International Jokes	30.00
☐ SMS Jokes	30.00
☐ Internet Jokes	30.00

MANOJ PUBLICATIONS
761, Main Road Burari, Delhi-110084.
Ph. No. : 27611116, 27611349   Fax : 27611546

RUCHI MEHTA'S COOK BOOK SERIES

- ☐ Dal Curries & Pulao — 40.00
- ☐ Ice Creams, Cakes & Puddings — 40.00
- ☐ Aaloo Paneer Dishes — 40.00
- ☐ Rajasthani Khaana — 40.00
- ☐ Pickles Chutenies & Murabbe — 40.00
- ☐ Vegetarian Cook Book — 40.00
- ☐ Punjabi Khaana — 40.00
- ☐ Breakfast Specialists — 40.00
- ☐ Laziz Mughalai Khaana — 40.00
- ☐ Delicious Soups — 40.00
- ☐ South Indian Food — 40.00
- ☐ Party Cooking — 40.00
- ☐ Tasty Snacks — 40.00
- ☐ Microwave Cooking — 40.00
- ☐ Chatpati Chaat — 40.00
- ☐ Non Vegetarian Food — 40.00
- ☐ Gujrati Dishes — 40.00
- ☐ Vegetarian Chinese Foods — 40.00
- ☐ Non Vegetarian Chinese Foods — 40.00
- ☐ Zero Oil Cooking — 40.00

MANOJ PUBLICATIONS
761, Main Road Burari, Delhi-110084.
Ph. No. : 27611116, 27611349   Fax : 27611546

Biographies of World Famous Personalities

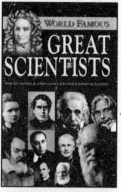

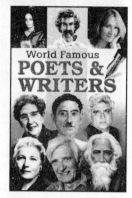

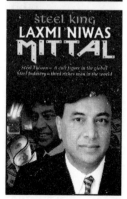

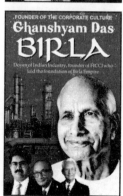

A *Treasure* *of Stories*
Specially for
CHILDREN

Big Size
Illustrated

❑ 101 Stories from Panchatantra	80.00
❑ Akbar Birbal Stories	80.00
❑ The Arabian Nights	80.00
❑ 101 Stories of Grand Mother	80.00
❑ Vikram Betal	80.00
❑ 101 Stories of Grandpa	80.00
❑ Aesop's Stories	80.00
❑ Jataka Tales	80.00
❑ Ramayana	80.00
❑ Mahabharata	80.00
❑ Fair Fair Fairy Tales	80.00
❑ Best Stories for Children	80.00
❑ Selected Stories from The Holy Bible	80.00
❑ Witty Tenali Rama	80.00
❑ Chandamama Stories	80.00
❑ The World's Most Popular Folk Tales	80.00
❑ Hillariously Funny Mulla Nasrudin	80.00
❑ Hitopadesh	80.00
❑ Shekhchilli	80.00
❑ Ghost Stories	80.00
❑ World Famous Adventure Stories	80.00
❑ Stories of Talisman	80.00
❑ Horror Stories	80.00
❑ Jungle Stories	80.00
❑ Sighansana Battisi	80.00

These Stories are not only engrossing but are also full of moral and social values

MANOJ PUBLICATIONS
761, Main Road Burari, Delhi-110084.
Ph. No. : 27611116, 27611349   Fax : 27611546
Mobile : 9868112194